Let's Go!
J love you forever,

Suz    12/25/89

Let's Go!
J love you forever,

NORTH COAST OF CRETE

"... out-jutting beaches thunder aloud to the backwash of the salt water"

— THE ILIAD, HOMER (RICHMOND LATTIMORE)

Page

| | | | |
|---|---|---|---|
| 55 | ROAD TO BASSAE, GREECE | 104 | ANEMONES, EPIDAURUS |
| 85 | PINE TREE, ALTAR OF ZEUS—PERGAMUM, TURKEY | 105 | SHRINE AND THEATER, EPIDAURUS |
| 86 | DETAIL OF GRIFFIN, TEMPLE COURTYARD, DIDYMA | 106 | TEMPLE AT BASSAE |
| 86 | TEMPLE—DIDYMA, TURKEY | 107 | FALLEN COLUMN, OLYMPIA |
| 87 | TEMPLE OF DIONYSUS, PERGAMUM | 108 | COLUMN RUINS, OLYMPIA |
| 87 | AESCULAPIAN SANCTUARY, PERGAMUM | 109 | REDBUD TREE IN GYMNASIUM, OLYMPIA |
| 88 | DETAIL OF ACROPOLIS, PERGAMUM | 110 | PROPYLAEA WITH VIEW OF PARTHENON |
| 89 | LIBRARY, EPHESUS | 111 | PARTHENON FROM INSIDE |
| 89 | ACANTHUS LEAF ON CORINTHIAN CAPITAL, EPHESUS | 112 | PARTHENON |
| 90 | THEATER, EPHESUS | 113 | PROPYLAEA |
| 91 | TEMPLE OF APHRODITE—APHRODISIAS, TURKEY | 114 | TEMPLE OF NIKE FROM PROPYLAEA |
| 92 | THEATER STEPS—LAODICIA, TURKEY | 115 | PORTICO OF CARYATIDS, ERECHTHEUM |
| 93 | STADIUM, APHRODISIAS | 116 | PARTHENON WITH DETAIL OF FRIEZE |
| 94 | OLIVE TREES IN THEATER—NYSSA, TURKEY | 117 | PORTICO OF ERECHTHEUM |
| 95 | TEMPLE OF ARTEMIS—SARDIS, TURKEY | 118 | TEMPLE OF APOLLO, CORINTH |
| 96 | AGORA WITH POPLAR TREES, APHRODISIAS | 119 | FOUNTAIN OF PYRENE, CORINTH |
| 97 | THEATER OF DIONYSUS, ATHENS | 120 | TEMPLE OF ATHENA, LINDOS |
| 97 | THEATER OF DIONYSUS, ATHENS | 121 | LINDOS |
| 97 | THEATER OF DIONYSUS, ATHENS | 122 | TEMPLE OF POSEIDON, SOUNIUN |
| 97 | THEATER OF DIONYSUS, ATHENS | 123 | TEMPLE OF POSEIDON, SOUNIUN |
| 98 | MARBLE THEATER STREET, EPHESUS | 124 | FALLEN COLUMN—NEMEA, GREECE |
| 99 | THEATER—PRIENE, TURKEY | 125 | THEATER AT MEGALOPOLIS, GREECE |
| 99 | THEATER—EPIDAURUS, GREECE | 126 | TEMPLE OF ZEUS—OLYMPIA, GREECE |
| 100 | THEATER—SYRACUSE, SICILY | 127 | A SECTION OF THE LION HUNT PEBBLE MOSAIC AT ALEXANDER'S PALACE—PELLA, MACEDONIA |
| 101 | THEATER OF APOLLO, DELPHI | | |
| 102 | THEATER—MILETUS, TURKEY | 128 | MYCENAEAN, STONE LION, DELOS |
| 103 | RUINS OF THEATER LODGING, EPIDAURUS | 129 | VINEYARD, CRETE |

THE ERECHTHEUM ON THE ACROPOLIS, ATHENS

"Athenians are lovers of beauty without having lost their taste for simplicity,
and lovers of wisdom without loss of manly vigor."

— THUCYDIDES (EDITH HAMILTON)

ROCKROSES, RHODES

# THE GREEK WORLD

No architecture has been able to explore the problems of being and action quite so forcefully or with such permanent particularity. The Greek was prepared to use his intellect both freely and with reverence upon the traditions of awe, joy and terror which he had inherited from the pre-rational ages. Expecting, most often, no immortal reward for proper action, he has moved to test the poignancy of human desires against the hard reality of nature's demands, saw both in strong, clear shapes and took nothing from the force of either. Believing himself to be unique, but at his best neither arrogant nor despairing in the circle of the world, he was able not only to conceive of the fundamental oneness, but to face the apparent separateness, of things. So the world he built, strictly selective though its elements were, was the world entire. In this he was aided by the special landscape which was his home, where movement always found its focus and variety its balance....

— Vincent Scully, *The Earth, the Temple and the Gods*

# PROLOGUE

When I first went to Greece I thought I was discovering everything at once, five things a day. My hunger for the monuments of antiquity, for museums, for people, for light and shade, for mountains, woods, islands, and seas, seemed to me insatiable. Indeed it never has been sated, but now I feel that I know Greece almost too well to write about it, and time meanwhile has washed away my footprints from those tracks. Greece has been the air I breathed and the life I lived, yet I can no longer easily recapture that younger self to whom it was strange. Nor can I quite shake him off, and I am afraid that he will dog the reader as he dogs me. Today I can answer nearly all of the naïve questions he began by asking, but he is still asking questions and I have lost my shame about his naïveté.

The continuous attraction of Greece for me has been something quite simple, and I am sure that I share it with many who will never write a book and some of those who have. It was the light, the physical sunlight. It was thyme-scented hillsides and plains of toasted thistles. It was the fragments of the marble architecture. It was spring at Pylos and at Souniun and in the Cretan mountains. It was the charcoal burners in the pinewoods and the donkeys and goats and anemones in the olive groves. It was autumn at Olympia, winter in the Arcadian mountains, the annual snowfall of wild cyclamen on the hill of Kronos. But above all it was the people. Most of the best friends I ever expect to have are Greek, and we have fifteen years of our lives in common.

15

But I came late to Greece, at the age of thirty-two, in 1963. I had started to learn ancient Greek as a schoolboy, at a school where Greek was hardly taught. All I knew about Greece then was the Elgin marbles, of which I treasured some sepia-tinted and forbidding postcards, and the fact that Oscar Wilde, who in the summer of my fourteenth year had just become my literary idol, said the Greek text of the Gospels was the most beautiful book in the world. So I demanded to learn Greek and changed schools in consequence. From that time I have never ceased to study the Greek language. There were some ups and downs, of course. One of the ups was Oxford, where I was lucky enough to be taught some medieval and modern as well as ancient Greek. There I discovered the few wonderful Byzantine writers. And there I discovered George Seferis. I venerated him then as an immensely great poet. Later I came to love him as a friend, almost as a father, and to respect and admire him more than I can express.

Coming so late in the day to Greece seemed at the time to be an impoverishment, but I take some consolation from hindsight. The terrible sufferings and the heroism and determination of the Greek people in their resistance to Hitler have transformed forever the way we look at Greece. Short of having known Greece before the war and fought through it in the Cretan mountains, as some of my English countrymen did, I prefer a Greece who knows herself, and whom we know, to all the privileges of prewar Europe, and I am glad not to have lived through the disasters of the two anti-communist civil wars that followed Hitler's war. On the other hand, I did live through the seven nasty years of the Colonels, from 1967 to 1974, and I am glad I was there. I am a witness to what happened, to the dignity and obstinacy of the Greeks, to their gallantry and their decency in a period of nightmare and of darkness.

My work in Greece was that of an archaeologist of some kind. I took part in excavations, but I spent some years translating and annotating Pausanias, who wrote in the second century A.D. a guide describing all the surviving monuments of ancient architecture and religion, and then many more years working at a full commentary on his writings in the light of modern archaeology. I chose him because of his reality, and because by studying Pausanias I could hope to know Greece as I longed to know it. The commentary is still unfinished, indeed hardly started, but I owe Pausanias a loyalty deeper than that of scholarship. Through him I got to know landscapes and sanctuaries and villages and mountains I

16

would not have seen otherwise. And work is peace after all; I have found it a resource in bad times and a pleasure in good.

The trouble was that my interest constantly spilled over, into the history of these same monuments in the Middle Ages, into the Greece of the first archaeological explorers, into modern and recent history, into the people among whom I was working, and finally into prehistory, which for years of obstinate stupidity I had resisted as an irrelevance. Perhaps the explanation was just that I had too many professions. From 1964 I was a Jesuit priest, but a priest without local duties. I taught the classics at Oxford, but I had to go abroad in winter, originally for reasons of bad health, so I took up classical archaeology. Yet the underlying condition and the force and momentum of my life were to be found in neither of these full-time professions but in poetry. And there was still my unending love affair with the Greek language; I also had an average educated curiosity about birds, flowers, and landscapes.

What I liked about Greek was not just poems and not just books but the impressive force of the language itself, unconfined by dictionaries, spoken in the streets, in cafés, and in the country. Greek has a longer continuous history than most languages; its written records go back nearly four thousand years, and its alterations in that time have been gradual and seldom ruinous. Under the Roman Empire, it was almost a world language. Under the Turkish Empire it sank back into its own roots and recovered what it had lost, the beautiful behavior, the suppleness and bite of country speech. In the last generation, poetry has been written in Greek as powerful, as memorable, and as individual as the best Russian or English-language poems of this century. The modern Greek language has hardly been charted; it can be learned only by listening. It has an astonishing range of tones and resources, and slowly learning and relearning to speak it has been one of the most satisfying pleasures in my life.

In the end I came to write poems of my own in Greek, not by choice, which would have been freakish and perverse, but when I had begun to dream and to think in Greek, and the pressure to poetry had become irresistible. The poems represent the furthest point for me of identification with what Lawrence Durrell calls "the distinctive form and signature of things Greek" without any loss of identity. The loss of one's national or professional identity in the pursuit of a love affair with a foreign country is always a mistake, I believe. There is something phony about "going native" anywhere in the world. Equally, of course, it is better not to amaze the inhabitants of another country with Bermuda shorts or a bowler hat, nor was I tempted to do so. I traveled in the wildest places I could find. I was a friendly bachelor. I drank deeply the wine of the country. But if ever anyone took me for a Greek, it was by chance, and only because so few foreigners speak the language.

After many years of study and of a monastic religious life, my first visits to Greece were like a delayed spring, a breaking of the ice. In 1965 I had just finished a long and often depressing course of training that had lasted seventeen years. It had included so many illnesses that the training itself seemed like an illness. Now the air glittered and smelled of leaves. I was both sophisticated and innocent, and I was very hungry for life. Greece treated me kindly. It was not a mythical or exactly a romantic place for me; what I was searching for and hungry for was reality. All reality was historical, I suppose; it always descends from history, and the history continues.

Greece has become so familiar to me that I am no longer able to get outside it, which would mean outside myself, except on rare occasions. It is like one of those old jackal-skin quilts that used to be so cheap in the Greek mountains, and so easy to find, if you happened to be there. You bought it long ago in the good days, and it still warms you. Now you know more life, and more about the Greeks and their sufferings, but it still warms you.

Later in this story, my first encounter with Eliot Porter's photographs felt like a slow, cold dawn. They are perfectly still and silent in almost all their subject matter. They have great visual beauty, great attraction of color and composition. Of course, his work has always had that, and also a dramatic quality, but here the dramatic sense is somehow frozen, as if it had combined with time itself, as if the landscape and the ruins were his own expression. This is a remarkable and, I think, subtle and passionate view of Greece; it could not be a young man's work. Mr. Porter's Greek photography began in the spring of 1967 just early enough to capture sites, especially the Parthenon, before they were destroyed or closed to public view. It is a personal love affair quite different from mine, but one that I respect and admire. Further, I submit that no finer, more coherent set of photographs of these subjects has ever been taken. These places have recovered in Eliot Porter's work a sharpness and a strength that had been lost since the fine engravings of the eighteenth century. They have regained their solitude and their intensity.

18

We have combined these photographs, more stately than any dreams, with a text that winds in and out of the same ruins and conveys, in the tones mostly of conversation, the world and the permanent power of the Greeks, the force of their effect on us and the precise detail of what happened to them. That was part of the history of nations, part of the progress of mankind. In the course of a few generations, one small, tough people, peasants and islanders mostly, produced an art that still has an influence, and an architecture of marble that in many ways is still exemplary. At the same time these people developed or created the secular theater, or laid its foundations. And they invented democracy and philosophy. Perhaps it is inevitable that those who developed democracy and philosophy would also discover tragedy and comedy. But even their science and medicine were not negligible. They calculated the size and weight of this planet. And most of the time they fought one another in a series of catastrophic wars.

This is all a very big mouthful. But Eliot Porter's work is profoundly disciplined. He is a subtle and distinguished artist. There is nothing obvious in his composition. He is one man, overpowering one moment. But by combining, by balancing one way of communicating against the other, we have hoped to convey, as simply but as fully as it can be conveyed, the Greek world. This book attempts to treat the emergence and history of the Greeks. It explains—in short compass—what happened to them; it conjures them up and makes them present, as they have been present to Eliot Porter and to me.

For most of us Greece is a world of imagination before it becomes reality. There is something childish, as well as something ancient and profound, about the way the Greeks imagined themselves, so that we accept Homer as a kind of second nature of mankind long before we learn to understand him. The Greece I used to imagine as a schoolboy was made up of old photographs; bits of *The Odyssey*; the endless, crashing boredom of Demosthenes learned by heart; some delicious, casual sentences of Plato; and the noise and smell of lawn mowers and cut grass outside the classroom windows. The way we pronounced ancient Greek at school made it a non-language, a comic invention. Tragedy was lost on me. I understood the severe and solemn rhythms, but it took us weeks and weeks to translate one play, at the climax of which an old lady, whose fury had filled our ears all through the spring season, was transformed into a dog. We felt it served her right.

19

Yet already I was hooked. There was already something more haunting about Hector under the walls of Troy and Odysseus in the cave with the nymph than about the other stories I knew. Since then I have spent a lifetime trying to pin down the special quality of the Greeks, and their nature, the special events that determined their history. The Elgin marbles and the Parthenon still make the same life-giving impression on me now that they did when I was fourteen. They are the same at any age. In the same way, fine photography of Greek architecture speaks directly, it abolishes distance and history. But Greece is a real place, and there are things to be said about it. History really happened, and any understanding that leaves history out is false.

When I left school, I knew that the walls of Troy existed, and they were high. I knew they had been excavated, and I could point to Troy on a map. But I had little idea what relation the real, excavated Troy had to *The Iliad*. Indeed, I am still rather doubtful about the question. What I find more interesting is the intermingling of imaginary and real worlds in the beginnings of all scholarship. I am certain that the Troy I imagined and still imagine owed more to *The Iliad* than it did to any excavation report. Helen was high on the battlements of "windy Troy." Yet its walls were gigantic, toppling, ruined, and Priam was a ruined king in a ruinous palace. That is not the picture that blind Homer intended.

On the other hand, I felt at that age as if the island and the cave where Odysseus lived with the nymph might exist as truly as the walls of Troy. One only had to go and discover. I think it was this mythical, summoning Greece, not the real Greece, that drew me in the end to dusty elephant-colored real mountains, and the mule droppings and the goat droppings and the olive trees and the water springs. The crispness of the ancient bronze and the crispness of the flowering anemones and wasted thistles belong to all those who search for them. They belong to those whose passion has entered reality. Perhaps all the deepest love affairs are in some sense imaginary; but Greece and its history are really there. They are less heady than Homer, but Greece is more profoundly intoxicating than written words.

Eliot Porter came to Greece with his own mature skill already developed. My own progress as a classical scholar was more haphazard. The landscape and the ruins that drew me aside to study Pausanias' more than seventeen-hundred-year-old guidebook in turn led me to spend more and more time in Greece, until I was more at home in the modern than the ancient Greek language. Throughout the fifteen years of this process, I continued to study the ancient writers, and they became more alive to me the further I strayed away from them into Greece itself.

That is one person's experience. No doubt both elements are necessary in different combinations for different people—the books and studies and libraries at one time, and the ruins and realities and the wild thyme and the chilly whitewashed taverns at another. Of course, it is not only the modern Greeks who have learned from ancient Greece. The city of Washington, D.C., has Greek roots; and it was proposed in the eighteenth century to make Greek, because it was the first language of freedom, the common official language of the United States. There is an irony in that, because the ancient Greek states, like the eighteenth-century United States, were slave-owning societies.

Still, there is a remarkable relevance in Greece today of the landscapes, and of many aspects of the way of life in the countryside, to the ancient world. It is amazing how much our own world has inherited from the early Greeks. It is also amazing what a strong sense of that vanished world, a world substantially dissolved into our own history and our own bloodstream, is still to be found in Greece itself. That has been one of the great surprises of my life. Where I thought to find my own romantic illusions I encountered realities more moving than any romantic ideas. But where I thought my scholarly understanding was most surely grounded I have often found myself deceived.

There are other countries, as well as Greece as it now is, where it is possible to learn important elements of the ancient world. One can learn the moral system of the honorable childhood of mankind, and the world view of nomadic herdsmen, anywhere from North Africa to Central Asia. One can study the permutations of Greek architecture all over Europe, and see the most thrilling Greek museum material all over America. But the country itself, with its special climate, its own sea, its unique limestone and marble geography, and above all its language and its ruins, still has something special to say, something genuine, something not said elsewhere.

In the tragedies of fifth-century Athens there is always a chorus. The chorus takes little part in the action; it speaks with timidity and pessimism, though often in verses of great beauty. Its advice is to accept, never to provoke the gods, to count any day a happy one if it was passed without tears. There is something terrible about the chorus. The members fill the street, they are the bystanders, and their ritual dances enclose all dramatic action. They are often the only survivors. They are timeless. They are like those old village women in black dresses who appear so miraculously today at every great local disaster, in every village in Greece.

That is an example of the survival of something stupefying and in its way terrible, a common factor of ancient and modern life. Those who still believe, as we all used to do, that the world can be altered for the better by our intervention believe really that they can alter the life of the chorus. By destroying mosquitoes, introducing fertilizers in the fields and con-traceptives in the villages, instituting political reforms and modern education, they will make the chorus disappear. Its traditional wisdom will be unnecessary, and tragedy itself will diminish. Medicine, the discourse of reason, and the rule of law will make inroads on it.

But that crusading feeling also goes back to the Greeks. Sophocles, the tragic poet, founded or helped to found the first great Athenian hospital. Plato was a severe critic of traditional wisdom and a social reformer on a frightening scale. We are lucky not to live in his utopia. The influence of the Greeks on us is on such a vast scale it is almost incalcu-lable, and most of it is luminous and fascinating. Much of the best in what we think of as our own reasoning, our own realism, even our own observation of nature, has its origin in their world.

No one can claim complete mastery over origins so ancient and so ramified. But Goethe said that a tradition does not truly belong to people until they have fought for it, and there is a certain truth in that. The truth about the Greek world belongs, I think, to anyone who is prepared to conceive of it and to imagine it right through, to confront it or to contemplate it. It belongs to us not in the measure of our scholarship but in the measure of our own depth, which I am inclined to think increases. Not everyone has the leisure or the talent to take a profes-sional course in this subject, but, all the same, the Greek world yields itself rather immediately to open minds and open eyes.

We need to remember that the ancient Greeks are different from ourselves. They are much tougher, and a primitive sap is still running vigorously in their lives. They are pagan, and they believe the gods to be sublimely beautiful, also in some ways hilariously funny, also ageless, sinister, and terrifying. The Greeks believe all this at once. Yet they are not at all close to psychological breakdown. Their cruelty, their avarice, their superstition, and their class war are by our standards extremely naïve. Their women are not liberated. Virility has an erotic glamour for their men as well as their women. The ancient Greeks from Homer to Aristotle know that in their world the brave die young, and they feel that the gallant physical courage of those whose quality dooms them so to die is the best and most beautiful thing in the world. All my life I have felt I am just at the beginning of understanding the Greeks.

Peter Levi

 # BEFORE HERODOTUS

Fifty or so miles northwest of Athens, a little off the main highway to Lamia, is the pass of Thermopylae. Literally translated, the name means "Hot Gates," and the hot springs to which it refers now support a spa for the treatment of rheumatism. But the etymology of the place has been overshadowed by history. It was here, on a summer's day in the year 480 B.C., that Leonidas, ruler of Sparta, with three hundred of his men, died in battle against an army of Persians under the command of Xerxes. Ten years before, under Darius, the Persian invaders had made an attempt to enter Greece at Marathon, just twenty-six miles from the center of Athens, and against all probability they had been turned back by a force of Athenians and Plataeans. Now, at Thermopylae, the Spartan defenders of the pass had refused to withdraw; in the end, betrayed and surrounded, they held their position and died there to the last man.

> *Tell them in Lacedaemon, passer-by,*
> *that here, obeying their command, we lie.* *

We have the story from Herodotus, who is often called the father of history. Though he did not really invent history—there are rudiments of it in the Bible, and in the archives and inscriptions

*Unless otherwise indicated, all translations are by the author.

24

of several ancient nations—he was unquestionably the first historian in our own sense of the word. He gives us the flavor of the scene through the eyes of a Persian spy:

> It happened that at this time the Spartans were outside their position. He saw some of them at exercise, and others combing their hair. He was amazed at what he saw, and discovered their numbers. When he had made his discoveries fully and for sure, he retired at his ease. No one pursued him, and he was treated with utter disregard.

The same word, *disregard*, is used for one of the heroes of the battle itself. Dieneces was told how when the arrows of the Persian army were loosed, the sky would be darkened by them. "And he was quite unperturbed, showing utter disregard for the numbers of the Persians, as if the stranger had brought him good news, since when the Persians darkened the sun one could fight in the shade, not in the heat. And they say this remark of Dieneces the Spartan, with others of the same kind, was left for their memorial." Herodotus calls Dieneces "best and bravest," the champion of the lost battle, and records the names of others who did well. He seems to have captured what happened just one moment before it became myth, or perhaps at that very moment of transformation.

The Spartans were a rear guard; they were commanded not to withdraw, and they stayed. It is also true that in the end they were surrounded, so the choice ceased to be real. But Herodotus loved them, for their defiance, their contemptuous throw-away courage, and their death. Generations have agreed with him, and so do I.

Herodotus was not a Spartan; he came from Halicarnassus, on the edge of Asia. But he was Greek in his ancestry, his attitudes, and his language. Greek connections with what is now the west coast of Turkey are very ancient; indeed, there was a continuous Greek population on that coast from about 1300 B.C.—centuries before the Spartan city-state itself was founded—until the early years of this century.

Who were the Greeks? If by this question we mean to ask where originally they came from, the answer is unclear and even now subject to revision. If we mean, rather, to ask what the Greek-speaking people had become by the fifth century B.C., when Sparta joined with Athens in fighting off the Persian invaders, the answer becomes relatively easy. "You Greeks," said an Egyptian to Herodotus, "are everlasting children." There was enough truth in

ENTRANCE HALL (SIR ARTHUR EVANS' RECONSTRUCTION)—
KNOSSOS, CRETE

In 1901 Sir Arthur Evans began to reveal the roots of Greek civilization
in Bronze Age Crete. The palace culture he unearthed
over twenty-five years of deep digs at Knossos was named Minoan
after Minos, stepfather of the ferocious Minotaur.

These late Bronze Age Minoan jars—approximately the height of
a grown man—were found in storage pits near the palace of Knossos.
Crete survived several earthquakes, including the volcanic destruction  ▷
of Thera, an island seventy miles north, which produced tidal waves
large enough to drown coastal settlements in the fifteenth or
sixteenth century B.C.  Knossos and Phaestus, on higher ground
inland, were spared.

STORAGE JARS AND FLOWERS, KNOSSOS

STAIRS, HAGIA TRIADA

COURTYARD—LATO, CRETE

GRAVECIRCLE, MYCENAE

It was Heinrich Schliemann, self-made German millionaire and dedicated nineteenth-century amateur,
who followed Homer's trail to Priam's city. "I could hardly control my emotion when I saw
before me the immense plain of Troy," he confessed, "whose image had hovered before me even in the
dreams of my earliest childhood." His next excavation was at Agamemnon's fateful Mycenae,
where close by the Lion Gate he discovered in 1876 the royal treasures within the Upper Grave Circle.

LION GATE, MYCENAE

The Mycenaean Greeks built castlelike fortifications at Mycenae and Homer's "Tiryns of the great walls."
By 1300 B.C. the Mycenaeans had prevailed over the Minoans at Crete and were the power
within the entire Aegean world. Mycenaean monarchy gave way first to the dark ages of the second
Dorian invasion, then to Greek aristocracy at Athens, to be followed by
Solon's fledgling democracy in 594 B.C.

RAMP TO BATTLEMENT, MYCENAE

BATTLEMENT, MYCENAE

"ODYSSEUS' BEACH," CORFU

Some suggest it was a beach like this one where the shipwrecked Odysseus was found by Nausicaä.

The Homeric epic tradition had its roots in history as revealed by the discovery here at Pylos in 1939 of clay tablets (deciphered in 1952) inscribed with the Minoan script, Linear B, an Achaean Greek language of Mycenaean times. Homer's Nestor, King of Pylos, furnished ninety vessels for the Trojan War, second only to Agamemnon's one hundred.

OLIVE TREES AND FLOWERS, PYLOS

IONIC CAPITAL, DELPHI

"The boundless sea resounded with an awful roar. The earth crashed with a huge boom. The wide heavens, shaken, groaned. From its base, high Olympus was made to tremble with the rush of gods. The deep quake reached dark Tartarus along with the tramping of feet, tremendous din of battle, and groaning wounds. Thus they hurled their roaring weapons at each other. The sound from both armies, calling out to each other, reached the starry heavens. They came together in a mighty battle cry."

— BATTLE BETWEEN THE GODS AND GIANTS, <u>THEOGONY,</u> HESIOD (SALLY WARDWELL)

DETAIL FROM FRIEZE, TREASURE HOUSE OF
THE SIPHIANS—DELPHI

TEMPLE AT AGRIGENTO, SICILY

RUINS—AGRIGENTO

tombs of the sort that were venerated at Mycenae. These were not the common dead but the landowning warlords who dominated the social system of Europe for three thousand years. Neither the innovations of Athenian democracy nor the imperial ambitions of the Persian invaders—not even the Roman Empire or the barbarian invasions it provoked—greatly modified this system, any more than they altered the dependence of all settled peoples on the practice of agriculture.

Like the practice of agriculture, the arts of the Bronze Age originated in Asia, arriving on the Greek mainland by way of the Minoan palace civilization in Crete. By the seventh and sixth centuries B.C. Greek-speaking mercenaries and adventurers had reached the shores of Palestine to the east and of Spain to the west. There were Greek colonies not only along the coast of Asia Minor but also on the Italian mainland and in Sicily, where they had already come into conflict with the seafaring Phoenicians, founders of the North African city of Carthage. Over the centuries, what had begun as trading enterprise or mere adventuring amounted to a national migration. Almost everywhere in the Greek-speaking world, but particularly in Asia Minor and in Sicily, power remained in the hands of the great warlords. The ruling dynasties founded by these men were noble rather than kingly, and did not last many generations. They built splendid monuments and were patrons of sculptors and poets; they competed for prestige at the great festivals held every four years at Olympia, at Delphi, on the Corinthian isthmus, and at Nemea on the Peloponnesus. They were not usually runners or boxers or wrestlers themselves, though their sons might be. Above all, as horse breeders, they desired to win the chariot race at Olympia. Prestige and public honor were their lifeblood. The great Olympic races went back into the past and into mythology. Homer had spoken of legendary games, and the eighth century B.C. had known real ones.

The Ionian Greeks of western Asia Minor were subdivided into six clans, four of whom were the same as the four clans of ancient Athens. One of these, the Neleidae, was respected as the founders of Miletus, a great trading port whose origins are hardly clearer than the many-layered history of Troy itself. The Cretans had settled there, and the Mycenaean wanderers had followed them. According to one tradition that has reached us, the Greeks married Carian women, who were native to the place; Homer refers to it as a Carian city. On the other hand, the German archaeologists who have worked at Miletus maintain that there was a pure, continuous stream of Greekness from Mycenaean into Roman times. Whatever the truth may be, of the importance of the city there is no doubt. Its wealth lay in the farmlands of the fertile Maeander valley, and in its harbor.

The traceable connections of Athens with Miletus and the rest of the Ionian cities of western Asia Minor are clear and unmistakable. Their dialect was the same, including the names of the months; they celebrated many of the same religious festivals. They had in common the tales and the language of Homer, who according to tradition was born in the Ionian city of Smyrna. But the influence of Homer, great as it was, only in part accounts for the flowering of Athens into what it became by the fifth century. For years I have pondered the various rival claims for explaining that miracle. Along with Homer, these include democracy, the invention of writing and of coinage, and some less definable, inborn quality of language and people. In the end I have come around to Ionian influences—above all the intense curiosity, combined with rational criticism and appraisal, that characterized the Ionian philosophers.

The intuitions of these men are the beginning of scientific speculation, and their naïve reasoning led in the end to scientific method, for all the rags and tatters of mythology that still clung about it. The obscure Pherecydes of Syros envisioned the world as a vast oak tree floating through Chaos; yet it is said that he died in the arms of the philosopher Pythagoras, who was probably one of his pupils. Thales, the earliest known student of geometry, lived at Miletus in the sixth century B.C. According to his theory, water was the material origin of all things: it was because the earth rested on water, and rocked or shook like a boat, that earthquakes occurred. A contemporary at Miletus was Anaximander, whose imaginative conceptions were at once grander and more subtle. His universe floated not on water but on the Unlimited and Everlasting; he envisioned the earth as the drum of a column, held in perfect equilibrium because all forces acted on it equally. Anaximander understood how rain was formed, and made a brave attempt at explaining thunder and lightning. He traced the outlines of the evolution of living species. Above all, he was certain that the world was intelligible, and he was apparently the first Greek to make a map—probably a relief cast in bronze.

A third contemporary at Miletus was the more earth-centered Anaximenes, who

61

pictured the earth as being flat as a tabletop, and the heavenly bodies as earthly exhalations. He explained the differences in the density of objects as a matter of rarefying and condensation of air, the single material underlying everything. A stone was air condensed; air at its most rarefied became fire. Such attempts to find a universal and intelligible explanation of everything material may be thought naïve or quixotic, but they are not stupid. Rather, they are the necessary beginnings of science.

Just as the sixth-century Ionian philosophers embody the supremacy of reason, their Athenian contemporary Solon is central to an understanding of democracy, a phenomenon that is likewise quintessentially Greek. He was born around 640 B.C., during the lifetimes of the earliest lyric poets whose works survive, Archilochus of Paros and Alcman, a native of Sparta. Solon himself was a poet, but of a very different kind. In some ways, indeed, he resembled the Ionian sages.

Solon first became famous at a time around 600 B.C., when Athens was at war with the neighboring city of Megara for possession of the island of Salamis. The war had been long and vexatious; when to many it appeared in fact hopeless, it was the poetry of Solon, chanted aloud, that rallied the Athenians to a final victory over Megara. Athens by then was a city torn to pieces by the conflict, decimated by hunger. The rich had grown richer, the poor poorer. Peasants had pawned their land and their own labor, even their own freedom. In the year 594 B.C. Solon was elected chief archon (or magistrate), and began putting into effect the reforms that turned Athens from a city half strangled by a ruling minority to a democracy under the most rational system of government ever devised. He abolished every debt for which land or liberty was the security, released the peasants from their appalling situation, restored their lands, and restored the freedom of those who had been enslaved. Foreign craftsmen were accepted as citizens; the systems of weights and measures, and of coinage—so far as it existed at the time—were reformed. He forbade the export of agricultural produce, except for olive oil. He created four classes, defined according to income, and designated the political responsibility of each. The lowest class would compose the general assembly, which in the course of a century or so would become the sovereign body of Athens. Members of the two upper classes were allotted the chief offices of state and a kind of Senate or House of Lords, which did not have enormous powers. The middle class controlled minor offices of state and a council of their own. Solon modified the severity of many laws, and guaranteed the right of appeal to a popular court, in effect diminishing the powers of the chief officers of state.

No such program of reforms can ever be instantly or perfectly successful, of course. There are bound to be dissatisfactions, and the weaknesses of any imposed system will show up under the strain of later disturbances. Solon himself lived to see some of those disturbances under the tyrant Pisistratus, whom he resisted in vain. But it may be said that liberty, fraternity, and equality as the foundations of government were the invention of a poet. The conception that guided his thinking was that the well-governed, the happy city has fair and equal laws, which are obeyed. It is an idea that goes back to *The Odyssey*. Hesiod made this abstraction a sister of Justice and Peace, and a daughter of Zeus; Alcman, more realistically, made it a daughter of Forethought. For Solon it seems to have been above all an inward quality in the life of the community, in the same sense that goodness is an inward quality. Solon's personal creed was simply expressed in one of his own poems:

> *Glorious daughters of Memory and Zeus,*
> *Pierian Muses, hear my prayer.*
> *Give me wealth, by the blessed gods, give me*
> *the high opinion of all mankind,*
> *make me sweet to friends, bitter to unfriends,*
> *to friends respected, unfriends terrible.*
> *I want to have riches, I do not want*
> *to get unjustly: justice always comes.*

These values are still related to the heroic world of Homer. Prestige is still paramount: this is the prayer not of a destitute peasant but of a nobleman who considers himself a fit ruler. What was implicit in Homer has become explicit in the public career of Solon. "May the great mother of the Olympian gods be my witness to this in the justice of time, dark Earth, whose boundaries fixed in many places I plucked up, who was a slave then and now is free. I brought back to Athens, to their god-built city, many who were sold, some unjustly, some justly, some runaways by the necessity of debt, no longer speaking the accent of Athens, long wanderers. Those who suffered the disgrace of slavery here, living in terror of the behavior of their masters, I set free."

What gives this speech its peculiar grandeur is surely a combination of the very old and the very new: the severity of ancient belief and the hardness of ancient life are the bone of it, and by contrast the newness of the justice Solon has envisioned is all the stronger. What he failed to do was inevitable: he was not able to produce a truly integrated society. But he is remembered now, as he was in his own Athens, as a sudden miraculous invasion of justice into human affairs, a thunderstroke of wisdom. Such memories are important in the history of every nation lucky enough to have given them a place.

Of the Greek temples whose remains are known to us, the earliest were dedicated to Hera, the consort of Zeus. One of the grandest of these was on the island of Samos, on a marshy spot within sight of the Asian mainland. It appears to have been rebuilt several times, on foundations dating to around the middle of the eighth century B.C. From what remains today it is still possible to envision the huge sanctuary, its pillared interior divided into two long aisles. In the dim light at the far end stood the cult statue of the goddess—a time-darkened piece of wood, said to have been miraculously discovered and perhaps already ancient when the temple itself was first built. Every year there would have been a ceremony during which the statue was dressed in fresh robes and hung with twigs from a kind of willow, the tree sacred to it. And just as the olive sacred to Athena grew on the holiest spot of the Acropolis, one of Hera's sacred trees grew immediately behind the altar, just outside the temple itself, where sacrificial offerings in honor of the goddess were burned.

Toward the end of the sixth century B.C. the rebuilding of the temple was begun on a still-grander scale, in keeping with the ambitions of the tyrants who ruled the island. In addition to encouraging artists and poets, it was the custom of the Greek tyrants to give their support to such public works. A tyrant was not quite the same thing as the kings of whom Homer wrote—not a patriarch but an autocrat, who most often came to power by means of a coup d'état.

At the time of Solon's reforms, no tyrant had succeeded in such a move at Athens. The attempt had been made, however, and Solon himself lived to see the eventual success of the tyrant Pisistratus, around 560 B.C. Twice exiled by his rivals, he nevertheless managed to leave the government of Athens to his two sons, Hippias and Hipparchus. The latter became known as a patron of the arts, but also for personal vices that led, in the year 514, to his assassination. Hippias himself was finally overthrown and sent into exile by the Alcmaeonidae with the help of the Spartans.

Modern scholars have tended to absolve the Greek tyrants, either because their historic role was felt to be inevitable in the circumstances, like the rise of fascism in Europe, or because of their patronage of poets and architects. But they were loathed by the Greeks, and it is not true that architecture or poetry depended upon them. *Tyranny* is close to being a word of blasphemy for the Greeks.

Polycrates of Samos, a contemporary of the Pisistratids, did more than any of them to give tyranny a bad name. Raiding and piracy had given him dominance over the eastern Aegean, and it was he who drove the philosopher Pythagoras from his native island. But like the Pisistratids he was a patron of poets—Anacreon was one of his favorites—and he carried on the rebuilding of the sanctuary of Hera that had begun under his father Aeaces.

By the beginning of the sixth century, temples all over Greece were being built of stone. It had not always been so. The first temple of Hera at Samos had limestone foundations, remains of which are still to be seen there; but the supporting pillars were of wood and have long since vanished. The Doric temples that were traditional in mainland Greece and (with a few subtle exceptions) to the west were versions in stone of something originally built in wood. Their huge capitals were like great cushions of stone, their pillars weighty, austere, harmonious, almost monotonous in their intensity. The capitals of the Ionic temples were elegantly curved like rams' horns, or like the stone buds of some flower opening in a way that is purely geometric. The pillars are sharp, fine, and stately, sometimes splendidly ornamented, the entire plan less rigid and more various. In both orders, the shapes had been gradually adapted and transformed, becoming more and more beautiful by a slow and consenting process that had been going on for two hundred years before they began to be built in marble.

The most famous of all the great sixth-century buildings of Ionia was the temple of Artemis at Ephesus—St. Paul's "Diana of the Ephesians." A huge building, it was also a masterpiece of rich and delicate workmanship. The shapes it embodied had come from the East, or from Egypt by way of the East, but here they had been analyzed and brought under control by long, rigorous mathematical meditations.

At Athens there were plans to build a similar temple, of a size unknown outside Ionia; but the fall of Hippias brought an end to the project. By then the Samian tyrant Polycrates had himself come to a dreadful end at the hands of the Persians. As Herodotus recorded it, Polycrates was lured by one Oroetes, a Persian governor of Sardis, to embark on an expedition during which he was murdered, and his dead body hung up on a cross. That was in the year 522 B.C. A year later, Darius I succeeded to the throne of the Great King of the Persians. In the year 510 he gave refuge to Hippias as an exile, and his quarrel with the Greeks began.

By the end of the sixth century, the Persian monarchy had concentrated such enormous resources of wealth, territory, and fighting force that "concentrated" is not a strong enough word to define Persian power. It now extended eastward to the Indus valley, southward into Egypt, and northwestward into Thrace on the mainland of Europe. Very few Persians can ever have seen both their eastern and their western borders. The outer territories were ruled by Persian governors, and under them by local noblemen—even, on occasion, by a local democracy. Members of ruling families were not notably loyal and had felt it no disgrace at all to hold power from the Persians, changing sides at will to do so.

Herodotus tells us that Samos, after the murder of Polycrates, was the first place to fall to the Persians. Darius, King of Kings, was a barbarian of an ugly kind, who crucified or burned his victims on a spit, destroyed the sanctuaries of gods, and marched out of his Asian headquarters flanked by pieces of a dismembered corpse. The Phoenicians, his subjects, were said to be addicted to human sacrifice.

In the year 500 the Ionian cities revolted against their Persian rulers. An envoy from Miletus appealed to the Athenians—who in refusing to take back Hippias, whom Darius hoped to install as Persian governor of Athens, had already shown hostility to Persia—for help, and a squadron of twenty ships sailed for Miletus. After a battle in which the Ionian forces were badly beaten, Herodotus as translated by Aubrey de Selincourt tells us, "the Athenians would have nothing more to do with the Ionian rebellion, and in spite of frequent appeals...refused to lift a finger....The Ionians, however, had already gone too far to retract, and continued their preparations for war against Darius....They sailed to the Hellespont and got control of Byzantium and all the other towns thereabouts, then, returning to the Aegean, succeeded in inducing the greater part of Caria to join them." An Ionian fleet assembled for the defense of Miletus, where the Persian forces were augmented by a Phoenician fleet, and was defeated. "The Persians now invested Miletus by land and sea. They dug saps under the walls, brought up artillery of all kinds, and...made themselves masters of the whole city....So Miletus was reduced to slavery....Most of the men were killed by the Persians...; the women and children were made slaves, and the temple at Didyma, both shrine and oracle, was plundered and burnt." The year was 494 B.C.

The fall of Miletus to the Persians was one of the greatest disasters in Greek history. It was also a turning point. If the Persian empire had overvaulted the Greeks, and extended its direct influence westward, the world would be the poorer. Certainly there was little beyond Greece at the beginning of the fifth century B.C. to stop a great military power. The consequences of three or four small battles—Marathon, Thermopylae, Salamis, Plataea—have affected the world ever since. If the Persians had not been stopped, but had taken over Greece, it seems likely that there would have been no Rome. Perhaps there would have been no Europe, and no United States.

# FIFTH-CENTURY ATHENS

The Athenian theater grew up with the Athenian democracy. Its childhood and its origins are obscure, and it was not until the fifth century that theatrical performances settled in the sanctuary below the Acropolis.

Nothing could look much simpler than an early classical theater. It was a circular dancing floor with a rock or two and a small building in the background, a few trees perhaps, and an altar. It looked just like a threshing floor. But it was half surrounded by a semicircle of wooden or stone benches, rising in tiers to accommodate the whole population of a city. The Theater of Dionysus at Athens has been estimated to have a seating capacity of from fourteen thousand to seventeen thousand persons; at times, quite probably, it held thousands more. Such numbers sound fantastic; but the theater's structure was such that it concentrated attention wonderfully on the area where the plays were performed. Every syllable spoken there could be heard. An empty theater even today lies under the sun rather tensely, as if it still awaited a messenger with the news of a famous murder.

At the beginning, Greek drama was connected with religious ceremony, in particular the worship of Dionysus. "It was performed to the end," according to David Grene and Richmond Lattimore, "on ground devoted to that god and before his priest; but developed tragedy did not have to be *about* Dionysus, and seldom was. Like most choral lyric, it was given through the medium of a formal competition. The early tragic poets drew, for narrative material and for metrical forms, on an already rich and highly developed tradition of non-dramatic poetry, epic and lyric. They also drew, no doubt, on the unwritten and almost inarticulate experience of a living people, on folk memory and folklore, cult and ritual and ceremony and passion play and mystery play. But tragedy did not grow out of such elements. It was *made*....Aeschylus himself, and his...contemporary Phrynicus before him, experimented with dramatic stories taken from contemporary history."

In the year 493 B.C. a play by Phrynicus on the fall of Miletus was produced at Athens. According to Herodotus, the distress caused by the event itself was still so profound that "the audience in the theater burst into tears, and the author was fined a thousand drachmae for reminding them of a disaster which touched them so closely. A law was subsequently passed forbidding anybody ever to put the play on the stage again."

In the year 476 Phrynicus offered another play with a theme from recent history, once again concerned with the Persian war. This time he used a chorus consisting of Phoenician women, and we know also—though the play has not survived—that the prologue contained a mention of the defeat at Salamis. Four years later Aeschylus offered a play of his own on the same subject. He had been twenty-four when the last tyrant was expelled from Athens, and in 490, at the age of thirty-four, he had himself fought against the Persians in the battle of Marathon. He had seen the founding of the Delian League, under Athenian leadership, and the growing confidence that had made the victories at Salamis and Plataea seem all the more splendid in retrospect. Like Phrynicus before him, Aeschylus set his play at Susa, the Persian capital. He presented as his hero the Persian King of Kings, lamented by the women of Persia. Tragedy itself not only permitted but forced him to show sympathy for that appalling collapse, for the Persian dead, and for the ruin of magnificence. The Athenians were shown as victorious and glorious, and that, apparently, satisfied them.

*The Persians* opens with gloomy forebodings, then the Queen's dream of disaster, finally the news of the battle in a messenger's speech. These messengers' speeches are important set pieces in all the tragedies that have survived. In *The Persians* the physical clash is described more realistically than anything in Herodotus, for all the formal setting of the play.

Aeschylus has already explained clearly the strategy and the layout of the two fleets, the night before the battle.

69

And when the light of the sun had perished
and night came on, the masters of the oar
and men at arms went down into the ships;
then line to line the longships passed the word,
and every one sailed in commanded line.
All that night long the captains of the ships
ordered the sea people at their stations.
The night went by, and still the Greek fleet
gave order for no secret sailing out.
But when the white horses of the daylight
took over the whole earth, clear to be seen,
the first noise was the Greeks shouting with joy,
like singing, like triumph, and then again
echoes rebounded from the island rocks.
The barbarians were afraid, our strategy
was lost, and there was no Greek panic in
that solemn battle-song they chanted then,
but battle-hunger, courage of spirit;
the trumpet's note set everything ablaze.
Suddenly by command their foaming oars
beat, beat in the deep of the salt water,
and all at once they were clear to be seen.
First the right wing in perfect order leading,
then the whole fleet followed out after them,
and one great voice was shouting in our ears:
"Sons of the Greeks, go forward, and set free
your fathers' country and set free your sons,
your wives, the holy places of your gods,
the monuments of your own ancestors,
now is the one battle for everything."
Our Persian voices answered roaring out,
and there was no time left before the clash.
Ships smashed their bronze beaks into ships,
it was a Greek ship in the first assault
that cut away the whole towering stern
from a Phoenician, and another rammed
timber into another. Still at first
the great flood of the Persian shipping held,
but multitudes of ships crammed up together,
no help could come from one to the other,
they smashed one another with brazen beaks,

70

*and the whole rowing fleet shattered itself.*
*So then the Greek fleet with a certain skill*
*ran inwards from a circle around us,*
*and the bottoms of ships were overturned,*
*there was no seawater in eyesight,*
*only wreckage and bodies of dead men,*
*and beaches and rocks all full of dead.*
*Whatever ships were left out of our fleet*
*rowed away in no order in panic.*
*The Greeks with broken oars and bits of wreck*
*smashed and shattered the men in the water*
*like tunny, like gaffed fish. One great scream*
*filled up all the sea's surface with lament,*
*until the eye of darkness took it all.*

Aeschylus still saw the world as Homer did. Sun and darkness are universal. Horror is horror, whoever suffers it. He had fought in this battle, an immense victory against odds, he was by no means a pacifist or a liberal; but there is something about him, hard to phrase in terms of our values, that I find more moving and more important than what we usually call humanism.

Aeschylus wrote seventy or eighty plays, of which we have seven, but three of those seven are a sequence, meant to be performed together: *Agamemnon, The Libation Carriers,* and *The Furies.* Taken together, these three plays are one of the most awe-inspiring works of art that the world has ever seen. Taken alone, *Agamemnon* is one of the greatest constructions of tragic poetry ever written.

We know less than we think we do about Greek dramatic production, and I must say that I have seldom seen an effective production of any Greek tragic play. What was conventional, expected, taken for granted by the Greeks looks gratuitous to us. It was Aeschylus who altered the convention of tragic plays from something much more archaic, by first employing two actors onstage together instead of one. The actors each wore a traditional mask, which rather formally represented the kind of character who was speaking. There was a chorus of twelve, which took some part in the action but also sang or chanted in lyric rhythms and performed a ritualized dance. In his poetry as in his dramatic structure,

71

Aeschylus is simple and bold, his language as clear and strong as whipcord, and his handling of set scenes is like the architecture of a fugue.

Tragedy is, among other things, a substitute for and a continuation of epic poetry. Its themes are mostly the same. The difference is in the huge, conscious, democratic audience. The chorus in a Greek tragedy almost always represents the people, speaking in proverbial language on questions that are nevertheless real to the audience. They are the women dressed in black or the old men on the harbor front. In the opening lines of the *Agamemnon*, spoken by a watchman on the palace roof, the situation described is one to which an audience for many of whom the events of the Persian Wars were an all-too-vivid memory would naturally respond:

*I ask the gods relief of these labors,*
*this watch from year's end to year's end, crouched*
*on the roof of the Atreidae like a dog.*
*I know the assembly of the night stars,*
*the bright lords glittering in upper air*
*that bring winter and summer to mankind.*
*I attend for the signal light to burn*
*and for the flame to blaze the news of Troy,*
*the city fallen. We are mastered here*
*by a woman's man-minded all-hoping heart.*
*While my night-restless bed gets wet with dew*
*and no dreams ever watch over my sleep,*
*because I must not shut my eyes and sleep,*
*when I think to sing or to hum a tune*
*pounding out song for a drug against sleep,*
*then I weep for the miseries of this house*
*that lacks the good management of the past.*
*O for lucky relief of these labors*
*and the fire of good news in the darkness!*
*O hail bright shiner, daylight at midnight,*
*beginning of dancing in all Argos!*
*Yooo! Yooo!*
*I signal clear to Agamemnon's wife*
*to come quickly from bed and raise her cry*
*in thanksgiving and welcome to this light,*

*because the city of Troy has fallen,*
*so says the messenger of fire at night.*

The chain of beacons signaling from Troy to Mycenae (though Aeschylus refers to it as Argos) is an image of great dramatic vigor. The reasons for the long, solemn buildup before Agamemnon himself appears—a buildup that never ceases to be dramatic, and that adds such vast dimensions to the murder that is the culmination of the play—must surely lie in the character and role of Clytemnestra, who commits that murder. Athens was not a liberal or permissive city in the middle of the fifth century, when the trilogy was produced. It was a very daring stroke to present this wicked, infuriated, and frightening woman as the central figure in a tragedy intended for the entire population. For Aeschylus it was essential to place the murder, itself a squalid event, in a context of intellectual seriousness and religious grandeur; otherwise I do not believe the Athenians would have stomached Clytemnestra. As it is, she becomes utterly convincing, much more so than Agamemnon himself.

In a tragedy such as this, the gods are inevitably on trial. Aeschylus saw it as his task to defend rather than attack the gods, but the consequences of Agamemnon's murder raise serious issues both for the gods and for men.

The hatred of Clytemnestra for her husband goes back to the killing of their daughter Iphigenia as the price of obtaining a fair wind for sailing toward Troy. Since then many things have happened, many other offenses against the gods; now, as one more insult to Clytemnestra herself, Agamemnon brings with him the Trojan princess Cassandra. For ten years Clytemnestra has never ceased to brood on the original offense against herself and the gods, the killing of her daughter. Cassandra, waiting motionless and silent through Clytemnestra's speech of welcome, remaining silent when the Queen addressed her directly, has foreseen everything that is to follow. She gives a cry; the chorus asks her to explain, and after a long, riddling dialogue she finally does so:

*I shall not speak in riddles anymore.*
*Be witnesses that I smell out swiftly*

73

*the track of evils that have been long done.*
*There is a choir that never leaves this roof,*
*unmusical, in concert, unholy.*
*And it has grown drunken and overbold*
*on human blood, it riots through the house,*
*unriddable, blood-cousins, the Furies.*

In an atmosphere of hysterical tension, smelling the stink of blood not yet shed, Cassandra enters the house and the murder of Agamemnon follows. The chorus is divided, uncertain what to do. Its speech is full of proverbial feelings, but at the end of this play, uniquely in Greek tragedy, the members are very close to actual, open rebellion: they take weapons in their hands. Here it is as though Aeschylus were giving expression to the instinct, if not the dogma, of direct democracy.

In *The Libation Carriers*, the second play of the trilogy, what Aeschylus offered his Athenian audience was something other than a simple revenge play. Orestes, the young hero, returns to Argos after many years, is welcomed by his sister Electra, and avenges the death of Agamemnon by the killing of his murderous mother and the usurper with whom she plotted his death. But almost at once he sees the Furies, whom no one else can see—the avenging spirits of his mother. Fleeing them, he runs away, first to Delphi, where Apollo clears him of guilt, then to Athens, with the gruesome creatures still in pursuit. Dreadful as they are, the Furies speak the language of archaic morality and archaic religion; in fact they are not unlike terrible old women, and they represent one strand in the beliefs and the psychology of Athens in their day. That is what Aeschylus confronts and transforms in the final play, whose chorus is made up of the Furies: he bridles them with religious authority, reversing a common formula of curses into a formula of blessings, and with legal institutions. The rights and wrongs of blood vengeance are to be decided by voting, and the terrible sanctities of the gods shall belong to an Athenian court of law. In the end it is Athena, casting the decisive ballot in his favor when the jury is deadlocked, who decides the fate of Orestes and persuades the Furies to accept an honored place among the deities of Athens.

Aeschylus does not shirk the difficult questions raised by the story he had chosen to tell. His answers might not have satisfied Voltaire, but they make powerful theater and

74

majestic poetry, which have a truth of their own. And they offer a vindication of the kind of government that prevailed in fifth-century Athens: one operated through publicly accountable, publicly appointed officials. What was done, what was decreed, how money was spent was now recorded on stones in public places, as a matter of perpetuity. The responsibility invoked by the outcome of *The Oresteia* is religious, legal, and human all at once.

Athenian power became very great in the lifetime of Aeschylus. He died in Gela, Sicily, in 456 B.C., only two or three years after *The Oresteia* was performed at Athens. The war with Persia had continued intermittently, as it would until 449—a fact that may have influenced the epitaph he wrote for himself:

> *Under this monument lies Aeschylus the Athenian,*
> *Euphorion's son, who died in the wheatlands of Gela. The grove*
> *of Marathon with its glories can speak of his valor in battle.*
> *The long-haired Persian remembers and can speak of it too.*
>
> —AESCHYLUS (DAVID GRENE/RICHMOND LATTIMORE)

That epitaph notwithstanding, it is as a dramatist rather than a soldier that Aeschylus is remembered now. One of the greatest passages in the plays that have come down to us occurs early in *Agamemnon* and is, I think, best rendered in prose:

> Zeus, whoever he is, if this is the name he likes to be called by, so I address him. I have nothing to liken to him, having weighed all things in the balance, but Zeus, if I must genuinely throw out of my thoughts their useless burdens.

> Nor shall he who was once great, swelling with boldness in all kinds of battle, nor shall he be reckoned, he is past; and he that was born then has met his thrower and is gone. But that man will hit the target of understanding, who rings out victory to Zeus, who set mankind on the road to understanding by laying down as universal law learning by suffering. The painful memory of grief trickles instead of sleep before the heart, and wisdom comes even to the unwilling. There is a sort of blessing of the gods, sitting by their force on the helmsman's fearful bench.

The final image of the helmsman's bench is obscure to us, but to Aeschylus it was part of

75

familiar experience. Perhaps a better English equivalent would be "taking their place by force at the helmsman's terrifying wheel." The phrase "a sort of blessing" might better be translated "There is, I think, a blessing." The word used is a sort of shrug, a "somehow," a gesture of uncertainty. It has no literal equivalent in our language, but is, like so much of Aeschylus—for all his grand and terrible universality—peculiarly Greek.

At the time the plays of Aeschylus were being produced in the Theater of Dionysus at the foot of the Acropolis, the splendid monuments that would one day crown the rock were still to come. Indeed, the building of the Parthenon, that supreme symbol of the greatness and daring of the Greeks, did not begin until nearly a decade after Aeschylus died. Great temples had been going up in Asia Minor and Italy for a century or more; at Olympia the Temple of Zeus, celebrated in antiquity as one of the Seven Wonders of the World, had been dedicated in the year 457. But the victory of the Parthenon is a victory of style, and of survival.

It was in the year 447, when peace had finally been made with Persia, that the decision was made to begin a program of building, in which Phidias was to be the overall designer and Ictinus the chief architect. Work then began, under Callicrates as contractor, on a temple to Athena, the patron deity of Athens. No great temple had ever stood on the crest of the Acropolis where the Parthenon now stands, though there are signs of an earlier, unfinished attempt, abandoned when the Persians destroyed the city. It was that appalling war that created the opportunity for a newly decorated Acropolis, for the harmony and the strength that we can still see in the ruins today.

The Parthenon was not built to stand alone. It was the crowning triumph of a monumental series of buildings that covered the whole rock—many statues and public inscriptions and altars and small sanctuaries. The entrance to the Acropolis was vast in itself and made of marble, as if to make clear that the whole Acropolis was consecrated. The solemn pillars of the entrance were built to be seen from the hill of the Areopagus, the assembly place of the sovereign people. Even though it remained faithful to a hundred traditional local rites of caves, trees, graves, special holy places, and ancient boundaries, the entire complex of the Acropolis was rationalized under Pericles and his architects to be an everlasting monument, the supreme self-expression of the Athenian people and the embodiment of the religion of the city of Athens.

Pericles was an aristocrat and a democrat. He was a member of the family of the Alcmaeonidae, active in politics by 462 B.C., and he became the popular leader of Athens. Archaeologists have pieced together in some detail the progress of the building on the Acropolis and have identified more than seventy-five different hands on the carving of the sculptures that made up the frieze of the Parthenon. Beginning in the southwest corner of the temple, it represented one of the city's greatest ceremonies, the Panathenaic procession that every four years brought a new sacred robe, the peplos, to Athena. Altogether the carvings showed more than four hundred human figures and more than two hundred animals. Undoubtedly that procession did, in real life, wind past the Parthenon. But the priest and priestess who stand among the gods are the servants of the ancient, doll-like wooden image of Athena, whose sanctuary had always been on the spot where the Erechtheum now stands. And it was to that wooden image—rather than to the monumental figure of Athena, made of marble, gold, and ivory, that was the central feature of the completed Parthenon—that the new robe was offered.

The marble statues that filled the huge west gable of the Parthenon represented the quarrel between Poseidon, god of the sea and earthquakes, and the goddess Athena, for the land of Attica. Poseidon struck the rock with his trident and seawater gushed out of it, but Athena drew from the rock the first olive tree. Both the olive tree and the print of Poseidon's trident were venerated on the Acropolis, and the ancient sanctuary we know as the Erechtheum was rebuilt soon after the Parthenon was completed.

The Parthenon itself was kept apart from the jumble of ancient sanctuaries that underlie the Erechtheum. It was meant for display, and to be overwhelming. The number of pillars on the east and west fronts were more numerous than is usual for a temple of this shape, in order to add to the impression of strength. The innermost rows of pillars, standing inside the walls of the temple, carried marble beams that in turn carried a second series of marble pillars. It will surprise the reader, as it continues to surprise me, that the description of these inner columns, which have perished, depends on a seventeenth-century traveler whose manuscript journal is still unpublished.

77

All this work cost money, which the Athenians acquired by imperial power. Archaeologists have uncovered detailed accounts of the tribute paid annually to Athens by the citizens of its empire over a period of forty years, from 454 to 415 B.C. According to a gazetteer produced by two American scholars, that empire included no fewer than 265 cities. Meticulous building accounts have been found showing, in the words of Paul MacKenrick, "that citizens, resident aliens, and slaves all worked side by side, and that all received equal pay for equal work. The achievements of Periclean Athens cannot be explained or dismissed by a scornful reference to 'slave labor.'"

Athens did nevertheless have its slaves, and like Greeks everywhere in those days the Athenians were quarrelsome, ruthless, and acquisitive. Only Athens among all the cities in the world came close to solving its own internal social problems, but Periclean Athens itself was hell-bent on self-destruction. It had become the leader, after the defeat of the Persians, of the new confederation known as the Delian League. Originally all the members of the league had an equal vote, and they met in council at the temple of Apollo on the island of Delos, where the common treasury was maintained. Things began to change after the death of Xerxes, when the Persians were no longer a threat, and the island of Naxos tried to detach itself from the league. Athens now took the lead in forcing Naxos to continue its allegiance— and its contributions to the treasury. A few years later, Thasos made a similar attempt, which was similarly foiled. From then on, Athens used force as well as persuasion to add new members to the confederation. In 454 B.C. word of a possible attack by the Persians became the Athenians' excuse to shift the treasury from Delos to Athens. Following this imperial move, the building went on, with occasional interruptions; in the theater, comedy as well as tragedy continued to flourish; but from 431 B.C. almost until the end of the century, Athens and Sparta, with various allies, were at war.

At the beginning of the Peloponnesian War, Aeschylus had been dead for a quarter of a century. Sophocles, his near-contemporary, was already sixty-five. Herodotus was in his fifties, and so was Euripides. Socrates was thirty-eight, Plato not yet born. The comic poet

Aristophanes was just seventeen. He had grown up while the Parthenon was being built, in the last glorious peacetime before the conflict began. Something of the atmosphere of peacetime Athens under Pericles entered deeply into him. For today's reader his words recall the brilliance of Vienna or of London just before the 1914 war. Most of what we praise in the quality of life at Athens, rightly or wrongly, is a reflection of Aristophanes' plays.

He began his work as a playwright in 427 B.C., with a play we no longer have. It must have been a grim year at Athens. Following the invasion of Attica by a Spartan army, there was plague at Athens. The epidemic continued from 430 through 428 and wiped out probably a quarter of the population. Pericles was one of those who died. As a defensive measure he had enclosed the area between Athens and the sea with long walls, turning it into one elongated shanty town for refugees; it was here that the plague had taken root. More than ever, the grandeur of the public buildings and the sacred quality of the countryside, with its scattering of holy groves, legendary trees and mounds, and small temples and statues, must have been in sharp contrast with the huts where the poor lived, let alone with the slave quarters. Small wonder that Aristophanes was to present life in the villages with such bittersweet nostalgia.

The conditions that brought Athenian comedy of the late fifth century into existence were more complicated than those that went into tragedy or, indeed, into democracy itself. But it had not strayed so very far from its ritual and folk origins about which we unfortunately know very little. And it can scarcely be overstressed that Aristophanes is only one fragment of a living tradition that has been lost. There were much earlier plays with animal choruses—the same wasps and frogs and birds that Aristophanes used. Since his particular Greek is a dead language, he is sometimes hard to unravel, and almost always impossible to translate. But the targets of the political attacks that characterize his plays—and that seem to have been his own contribution—are often clear enough.

Sometimes the entire plot of a play by Aristophanes has a political edge. The *Acharnians*, produced in 425, is about peasants longing for peace, and notwithstanding certain devastating remarks the play is friendly toward its characters. In *The Knights* of a year later, the young aristocrats of the city, those whose fathers could afford to maintain a horse and its equipment, sing hymns to Athena and to Poseidon. The lyrics Aristophanes gives them are as crisp and elegant as the white marble riders that are among the figures along the frieze of the Parthenon. On them he lavishes the traditional sentiment that youth and gaiety have always inspired: they are young and gallant, the flower and hope of the city, who are serving their country and likely enough to die doing it. But Aristophanes mocked everybody, including (in *The Clouds*, produced in 423) his good friend Socrates.

In *The Knights* an oracle has just foretold that Athens will be ruled someday by a sausage-seller. At that moment one enters and is greeted with enthusiasm.

> DEMOSTHENES: *Dear Sausage-seller, rise, our Saviour and the State's.*
> SAUSAGE-SELLER: *What's that you say?*
> DEMOSTHENES:                                 *O happy man and rich!*
>     *Nothing today, tomorrow everything*
>     *O Lord of Athens, blest throughout!*
> SAUSAGE-SELLER:                           *I see, sir,*
>     *That you must have your joke, But as for me,*
>     *I've got to wash the guts and sell my sausage.*

—EDITH HAMILTON

Although we think of Aristophanes as the essential Athenian—and happy Athens if that was so—such characters as his sausage-seller may tempt one to doubt it. Such a low-life character might come from any small city with a market and would be hard to fit into a Socratic dialogue. The peasants have their equivalent in rustic comedy; Shakespeare certainly knew them. The appalling politicians and some of the other minor characters are more specialized, but the world of everyday Athens that Aristophanes suggests is in fact strange to us. The most alien thing about it is the institution of slavery, by which the city lived. Comic slaves have no more relation to life than comic Socrates, lost in the clouds.

> FATHER:                                   *Tell me, please,*
>     *What are you doing up there in a basket?*
> SOCRATES: *I walk on air and contemplate the sun.*
>     *I could not search into celestial matters*

80

Comedy transforms the world as no other art can do, and we conspire to be pleased with it. Mozart's operas act in the same way. In Aristophanes the transformation has a certain formality; the plots have a touch of ritual. In *The Knights* the leaders of the state appear as slaves of Demos, the People. Demos is a clever old man in difficulties with his tricky household. In the transformation, Demos is boiled in a pot and emerges with his youth renewed and a new, wise adviser. He is Athens itself in its glory, a king among Greeks.

The war continued to go badly for Athens. Plataea fell to the Spartans, followed by Olynthus and Amphipolis, where Pericles' successor, Cleon, was killed in battle. A peace arranged by Nicias, the new Athenian leader, in 421 amounted to a stalemate—though Aristophanes defended it in the comedy called *Peace*, performed that same year. The chief rival of Nicias was Alcibiades, who in 418 led an unsuccessful revolt by a coalition against Sparta. Two years later, he was a leader in the sack of the island of Melos, after its citizens, who wished to remain neutral, had refused to join the Athenian coalition. A year later came the expedition to Sicily, which was to end in disaster. Alcibiades and Nicias were both involved as commanders. Recalled to Athens to face a charge of sacrilege, Alcibiades deserted to the Spartan side of the original conflict, and the fleet under Nicias was overwhelmed, with enormous losses. With help from the Persians, the landlocked Spartans began building a fleet of their own.

The chronicler of these events was Thucydides, whose lifetime overlapped with that of Herodotus but whose method as a historian was altogether different. Whereas Herodotus was amiably devious and unsystematic, Thucydides' entire history of the Peloponnesian War is highly organized, with an accuracy of phrasing, a sobriety of conception, a candor, and a laboriousness that make it in its own way a very great work. Born in Athens around the middle of the fifth century, Thucydides held a military command at Amphipolis in 424, and for having failed to prevent the surrender of that city to the Spartans he was exiled until the end of the war. When the war ended, he came home, but he died without finishing his history. The concision and roughness of his language make him difficult to read; but in the seventeenth century he encountered—or so it seems to me—the perfect translator in Thomas Hobbes, whose stylized prose marks out each successive stage of the disaster at Syracuse like a drumbeat:

> After this cruel battle, and many galleys and men on either side consumed, the Syracusans and their confederates having the victory took up the wreck and bodies of their dead, and returning into the city erected a trophy. But the Athenians, in respect of the greatness of their present loss, never thought upon asking leave to take up their dead or wreck, but fell immediately to consultation how to be gone the same night.

> And Demosthenes coming unto Nicias delivered his opinion for going once again aboard, and forcing the passage if it were possible betimes the next morning; saying that their galleys which were yet remaining and serviceable were more than those of the enemy. (For the Athenians had yet left them about sixty, and the Syracusans under fifty.) But when Nicias approved the advice and would have manned the galleys, the mariners refused to go aboard, as being not only dejected with their defeat but also without opinion of ever having the upper hand any more. Whereupon they now resolved all to make their retreat by land....

At Athens, the response of Aristophanes to the Sicilian expedition was to write the most magical of all his plays, *The Birds*. It concerns two Athenians who wander off and help the birds found a city. The long lyric in which the birds are summoned is interspersed with bird noises of convincing brio, and the play ends with a sacred marriage, Zeus having been brought to terms with those below—everything, in short, having been reconciled. Following the disaster at Syracuse came *Lysistrata*, one of the strongest and funniest of all the plays of Aristophanes, about an international conspiracy of women to refuse sex to their men until the men make peace.

In his own way the tragic poet Euripides had been making the same statement.

82

*The Trojan Women*, produced in 415, is one of several stark treatments of the fate of prisoners at the fall of Troy, in which Euripides, horrified by the events of his own time, expressed what many of his audience must have half felt but been inhibited from saying.

There was a general revolt in the year 412 by the dependencies of Athens. Among them was Miletus, which had been turned into a garrison before it had quite recovered from its destruction by the Persians. A year later, Alcibiades once again switched sides, and the party of the oligarchs brought him back to Athens. He was not in power for long, but with a burst of what looks like insane optimism the work of building the Erechtheum was resumed. So, apparently, was the adornment of the little Temple of Athena Nike at the entrance to the Acropolis—including a frieze of exquisitely carved figures of Victory along the balustrade, of which the most famous (now to be seen in the Athens Museum) is shown pausing to adjust her sandal. The irony is too complex, almost, to bear thinking of.

Whereas on land the Spartans in force were more or less invincible, the Athenians had remained confident of holding the sea against them. But then the Spartans built a fleet, enlisted the aid of the Persians, and won a major naval battle. The outraged opponents of Alcibiades banded together and drove him from Athens, this time forever. In 406, confident because of winning another battle at sea, the Athenians once again declined an offer of peace.

The story of these campaigns is one of appalling folly, and of great bravery that somehow makes it worse. The war had taken on a logic of its own. Neither side could bear to see its interest threatened. The Athenians had grown hysterically fearful of the loss of allies, and what had once been a free alliance of equals against Persia became a garrisoned empire with savage punitive expeditions. The aggressive Spartans, like the aggressive Germany of 1914, feared being encircled. Peace was attainable more than once, but peace was despised, and no one in the sphere of conflict was permitted to be neutral. We do not know what Greece might have become, above all what Athens might have become, if peace had been made.

The war ended in 404 B.C., with the dismantling of the walls of Athens to the music of Spartan flutes. The Spartans had needed no walls of their own: no foreign army could penetrate their rock-protected valley, and all their wars had been fought abroad. Sophocles, whose long career had spanned almost the entire fifth century, did not quite live to see the fall of Athens. Neither did Euripides, who in 408 had left the city—perhaps for political reasons—and spent the last two years of his life at the court of Macedonia. Sophocles outlived him just long enough to appear in mourning for him at the Theater of Dionysus, in the last theatrical festival of his own life.

PINE TREE, ALTAR OF ZEUS—PERGAMUM, TURKEY

"Being human, you may not say what will happen tomorrow.
Nor, seeing a man blessed with wealth,
    how much time he has left.
For not even so swift is the shifting
    of a fly's outstretched wing."
— SIMONIDES

DETAIL OF ACROPOLIS, PERGAMUM

LIBRARY, EPHESUS

"If, therefore, you are skilled in Homer, and if, as I've just said,
having held out a promise that you would demonstrate that skill,
you cheat me, then you are unjust. But if you are not skilled, but,
as I've proposed, are possessed by divine providence and,
knowing nothing of Homer, still say all those beautiful things
about the poet, then you are not unjust. Choose then which you prefer
to have me think: that you are an unjust man or divinely inspired."

— SOCRATES TO ION OF EPHESUS, ION, PLATO (SALLY WARDWELL)

ACANTHUS LEAF ON CORINTHIAN CAPITAL,
EPHESUS

AGORA WITH POPLAR TREES, APHRODISIAS

Theater was the popular medium; through it philosophical ideas and teachings percolated to a mass audience. M. I. Finley in *The Ancient Greeks* writes: "Obviously, some men departed from the Theater of Dionysus solemnly saying to their friends, in whatever was the contemporary idiomatic equivalent, 'it makes you think.'"

THEATER OF DIONYSUS, ATHENS

MARBLE THEATER STREET, EPHESUS

The tragic dramatists were committed to historic myths—especially those based on minor characters and events of the Trojan War—to stir large audiences. The plays were of direct, consuming relevance to the fifth-century theater-goer, even though many of the stories were then six or seven hundred years old.

"Euripides wrote shockers, and it is not enough to say that this was because he was an innovator. He was, but so were his predecessors. Aeschylus was more daring, drastic, and original; Sophocles was no serene and static classicist. Perhaps the most significant remark about Euripides and Sophocles is one supposed to have been made by Sophocles, that he himself showed men as they ought to be (or as one ought to show them) but Euripides showed them as they actually were. He is the father of the romantic comedy, the problem play. There has never been anyone else like him."

— EURIPIDES I, RICHMOND LATTIMORE

THEATER—PRIENE, TURKEY                    THEATER—EPIDAURUS, GREECE

Thucydides writes sparingly of Athenian youths who conquered Sicily only to die as slaves in stone quarries near Syracuse following Alcibiades' blunder in 414 B.C.: "Having done what men could, they suffered what men must."

THEATER—SYRACUSE, SICILY

"The theater is of local limestone and could seat about 5,000. The first one was built on the site, facing the valley and dominating the entire precinct, at least by the early years of the third century. Its present state is that of the rebuilding about 160 B.C., with some later modifications in details."

— THE ANCIENT GREEKS, M. I. FINLEY

THEATER OF APOLLO, DELPHI

TEMPLE AT BASSAE

The earth spirit at Olympia, according to Pindar, was Zeus' grandson, Pelops, who gave his name to the Peloponnesus. Before the Olympic Games were first celebrated in 776 B.C., Olympia was a religious center for farmers. Even after the Doric temple of Zeus was completed by an Elean architect in 456 B.C., Pelops continued to be worshiped in the vicinity. The Olympic Games were banned by a Byzantine emperor in A.D. 393; the temple was devastated by an earthquake two hundred years later.

FALLEN COLUMN, OLYMPIA

PARTHENON WITH DETAIL OF FRIEZE

PORTICO OF ERECHTHEUM

The Erechtheum, a temple dedicated jointly to Athena and Poseidon-Erechtheus, is located on
the site of the legendary contest between the two gods and was completed in 404 B.C., the date also
of Athens' defeat by Sparta that marked the end of democracy in classical Greece.

"The time for extracting a lesson from history is always at hand for those who are wise."

— DEMOSTHENES

TEMPLE OF APOLLO, CORINTH

FOUNTAIN OF PYRENE, CORINTH

TEMPLE OF ATHENA, LINDOS

"Look well at this, and speak no towering word
Yourself against the gods, nor walk too grandly
Because your hand is weightier than another's,
Or your great wealth deeper founded. One short day
Inclines the balance of all human things
To sink or rise again. Know that the gods
Love men of steady sense and hate the proud."

— FROM ATHENA'S SPEECH, <u>AJAX</u>, SOPHOCLES (JOHN MOORE)

LINDOS

"I once remarked to a painter how helpful I found a remark of Cezanne,
that the sky is not blue color but blue light. He answered that nothing is a color,
everything we see is light. That is particularly true of Greek landscape."

— <u>THE HILL OF KRONOS</u>, PETER LEVI

121

TEMPLE OF POSEIDON, SOUNIUN

"The right time for men's sailing is fifty days after the sun's turning, when the season of
wearying heat has come to an end. Then you will not shatter your ships nor will the sea destroy
your men, unless Poseidon, Earthshaker has it in mind, or Zeus, king of the gods, wants
to kill them. For the fulfillment of good and evil alike are theirs."

— <u>WORKS AND DAYS</u>, HESIOD (SALLY WARDWELL)

TEMPLE OF POSEIDON, SOUNIUN

The description of that bad end, in the speech of another messenger, is one of the master-pieces of Greek tragic poetry. The first voice is that of the god:

> *"I bring you him who put to ridicule*
> *me and my mysteries. Take your vengeance."*
> *And as he spoke one flash of dreadful light*
> *struck at the earth and struck against heaven.*
> *The air was silent. The wooded ravine*
> *held all its leaves silent. No creature called.*
> *Their ears had not received that voice clearly,*
> *they stood still, and they moved only their eyes.*
> *And again he commanded, and when they*
> *knew the clear order of the Bacchic god...*

In appalling detail, the messenger describes how Pentheus is torn to pieces by the women. There follows an even more horrifying climax as Agave, the mother of Pentheus, comes back to Thebes carrying the head of her son. The god still possesses her, and she believes the head to be an animal's. The play ends with her frightful return to sobriety, in verse of masterful simplicity that leads, step by infallible step, to the moment when old Cadmus recognizes the head of Pentheus in the hands of the mother: "O grief not to be measured or looked on."

Euripides did not live to see *The Bacchae* produced at Athens, in the year 405 B.C. In his lifetime he had not been very popular. He had taken no part in the life of the state, except once to serve on an embassy. He had been bookish, when bookishness was rare. He was an intellectual in the modern sense, a conscious progressive. His influence after his death was immeasurable. It extended into comedy, into romance, even into the literature of the Christian Church: the lives of the martyrs were written under his direct influence. He introduced a new realism into the tragic theater, whose structure was beginning to break up while Athens itself fell apart.

The last play of Sophocles, *Oedipus at Colonus,* was also posthumously pro-duced. It had been written as the shadows fell at Athens. The Spartans were visible in the fields; the city was under siege and had already suffered drastic evils at home and abroad. His long life had spanned almost the entire fifth century. He had been a boy when Aeschylus fought the Persians, and had led the dancers at the celebration of victory at Salamis. He was also a musician and had at first acted in his own plays. In 468, when he was about twenty-eight, he won a prize for tragedy against Aeschylus. Altogether he wrote no fewer than 123 plays, of which we have seven, plus the ruins of one satyr play. His reputation, as a writer and a man, seems always to have been unassailable. He held office as state treasurer, he served twice as a general, and he was a member of the state commission whose task it was to deal with the crisis of the Athenian defeat in Sicily.

Throughout his plays, Sophocles is the spokesman for the blackest tragic view of mankind. He had been a soldier, and the *Philoctetes* and the *Oedipus Rex* deal incomparably with the experience of physical pain. He knew just what effect he intended, and those effects were calculated and produced with a powerful economy. Brought up with the Athenian theater as a living institution, he reflected the experience of life and the actual sayings of people in the street; but the construction of his plays held these elements more exactly in place than tragedy had ever done before or would ever do again.

One of the constant themes of Sophocles is the fulfillment of prophecy. Watching *Oedipus Rex*, the Athenian audience knew that Laius had been doomed to be killed by his own son, Oedipus. *Oedipus at Colonus* is likewise impregnated with prophecy. The play concerns the old blind King's death, his mysterious disappearance into the earth at a prophesied place, in a sacred wood of trees near Athens. Looking down from the Acropolis, you can still see the place where that wood was.

> ...if accidents can be inspired it is by an inspired accident (that) Athenian tragedy passes from our ken in Attica itself, and with Oedipus; at Colonus the birthplace of Sophocles, not two miles from the Theatre of Dionysus. Here is the Unity of Place. "And the place is holy."
>
> —GREEK TRAGEDY, H. D. F. KITTO

The connection between a man doomed, greatly afflicted by the gods, and a holy man, particularly a holy dead man, is close and automatic in Greek religious thinking. The terrible crime and the beggar's wandering to which Oedipus was predestined created, the Greeks instinctively felt, a sort of sanctity. At the beginning there are constant references to the sacred wood; the words of Oedipus and his daughter Antigone, those of the first Athenian they meet, and those of the disturbed chorus, who want the exile removed from this place, build up its sacredness and mystery. Antigone first describes it:

> This is a holy place, all overgrown
> with laurels, vines and olives, the quick-winged
> nightingales are singing inside the wood.

The Athenian stranger's first words are: "Before you tell me more, move from that place. It is unholy to walk where you are." We are told of the gods of the wood, of Poseidon and Prometheus; the place is called the bronze-footed road, the defense of Athens, the territory of the mythical heroic horseman Colonus. When Oedipus discovers where he is, he breaks out into passionate prayer: "O terrible-eyed goddesses—" because this is where he is destined to die and be at peace. "Come you sweet daughters of the ancient Dark..."

More than a third of the way through the play, when Theseus, King of Athens, has accepted the presence and mission of Oedipus, the chorus bursts into one of the most beautiful lyrics in Greek tragedy. Yeats translated them with a greatness of his own:

> ...yonder in the gymnasts' garden thrives
> The self-sown, self-begotten shape that gives
> ·Athenian intellect its mastery.
> Even the grey-leaved olive-tree
> Miracle-bred out of the living stone;
> Nor accident of peace nor war
> Shall wither that old marvel, for
> The great grey-eyed Athena stares thereon.
>
> Who comes into this country, and has come
> Where golden crocus and narcissus bloom,
> Where the Great Mother, mourning for her daughter
> And beauty-drunken by the water
> Glittering among grey-leaved olive-trees,
> Has plucked a flower and sung her loss;
> Who finds abounding Cephisus
> Has found the loveliest spectacle there is.

134

These famous lyrics are only one stone among many in the austere architecture of the play. Their dramatic force is that they beautifully settle the nature of the holy place. What happens is dark and terrible, but it has another aspect that after this is almost obvious, expected. The verses, in fact, in some ways resemble those of comedy—in their intense local feeling, their sheer beauty, and their sunny religious patriotism they could be matched by Aristophanes. The wood remains mysterious, and most of Sophocles is dark, as is so much of this play. Yet in its despairing hopefulness, wringing some goodness out of religion as the olive sprouted from the rock, it must, I think, express the aging Sophocles more fully than his early works. Knowing that Colonus was his birthplace, we can even see in it a kind of self-portrait.

For me the most fascinating episode of all in the public life of Sophocles is one that took place during the Peloponnesian War, when he served as priest of the healing god Aesculapius, whose cult was introduced at Athens in 420 B.C., following the peace of Nicias. The primary seat of the god of healing was at Epidaurus. Extensive excavations there have uncovered, not far from the theater, a temple of Aesculapius and a complex of buildings that included a dormitory to house the patients who had traveled there in hope of being cured of disease. Along with building accounts, archaeologists have found a record of forty-three miraculous cures. Nowadays a Greek in search of such a cure would make a pilgrimage to the shrine of the Virgin of Tenos, where the scene—with its lit tapers and votive offerings, and the sleeping forms of those hoping for a miracle—is probably much like the one at Epidaurus in ancient times, except that there is no sign of the snakes associated with the worship of Aesculapius. (They have come down to us in the form of the caduceus, the symbol of the medical profession.) While the sanctuary of the god was being built at Athens, Sophocles dedicated his own house to the god and kept there the necessary sacred snake. For this he was venerated at his death as Dexion, the receiver of the god.

The temple of Aesculapius was on the southern slopes of the Acropolis, where its ruins are still to be seen. The cave of the water spring of the god, which later became a Christian baptistry, is to my mind one of the eeriest—I might say the naturally holiest or most haunted—of all the surviving shrines of Greece. But the temple cult had come from Epidaurus, and although it was surrounded by and permeated with visions and miracles, this was the most progressive and effective hospital system in Greece—and possibly in the world. We know from the instruments recovered by archaeologists at Epidaurus that the successful methods of cure included surgery. It seems to me a significant comment on the character of Sophocles as a poet that he also founded a hospital.

After *Oedipus at Colonus,* tragedy continued to be written as well as performed, but the force had gone out of it: I do not know a single good line of tragic verse written after 400 B.C.—at least, not in ancient Greek. Comedy transferred its affections to a new, duller, more refined audience, and was altered in that process. Aristophanes himself lived through the fall of Athens and the changes that came in its wake. By the time of his last surviving play, the Athenian comic chorus had withered to nothing. In the most serious of Aristophanes' surviving plays, *The Frogs*—produced at Athens in the same year as *The Bacchae*—the animal chorus is exploited with all the hilarity and gusto of *The Birds,* and the noises made by the frogs are even funnier.

Athenian comedy very often satirized tragic poetry—the favored target, though not the only one, being Euripides. In *The Frogs* the last great tragedians are dead, and Dionysus descends to the underworld to judge between Euripides and Aeschylus and to bring back one of them alive, for the purpose of restoring dramatic art in Athens. The seriousness of the play is not in the contest between the poets—which, though fascinating, is meant to be played for laughs—but in the underworld itself, the mysterious singing of the immortal dead who were initiated in their lifetimes into the sacrament, if one may call it that, of the mysteries at Eleusis. (When Alcibiades was relieved of his command and recalled to Athens at the time of the Sicilian expedition, it was because a drunken prank in which he was involved had been exaggerated by his enemies into a profanation of those mysteries. To this day we have only hints about the nature of what went on in the sanctuary at Eleusis, other than that it was a reenactment of the story of Demeter and the abduction of her daughter, Persephone (or Core) by the god of the underworld.)

The seriousness of *The Frogs* lies also in the pessimism and nostalgia that had seeped into the bones of the play. Some of this may derive from a lost play by Eupolis, possibly a better one than *The Frogs,* in which the chorus consisted of the small towns of Attica personified as heroes of the underworld. It was Aristophanes who introduced the chorus of frogs, the mysterious singing, and most of the jokes. But the earlier conception must have been closer to the reality of what was happening. The fall of Athens was visibly coming in those years, and comedy could not but reflect it.

Whatever happened to Aristophanes in his lifetime, the last play of his that we have, and one of the last he wrote, shows his high spirits undiminished. The *Plutus,* produced in 388 B.C., may possibly be no more than an adaptation of a lost play by the same name that had been produced twenty years before. Aristophanes held state office early in the fourth century, and the quality of his criticism of individuals and of policies gives us no reason to think that he was ever deeply embittered with anything at Athens. The plot of *Plutus* concerns the blind god of wealth, who is advised by the Delphic oracle to go and get his sight restored by Aesculapius at his shrine on the slopes of the Acropolis. A few scholars, of whom I am one, count this among Aristophanes' most thrilling plays. I am unable to think of him without remembering the grim moment when the young gigolo gets wealth and the rich old woman is left alone—a moment of pathos such as occurs also in *Lysistrata.* It is the tour de force of an old and experienced comic poet.

The earlier Aristophanes represents a moment of unique fascination: a fragile and vulnerable art spun out of the same whirligig of influences and events and contradictions that would soon destroy it. There is something gleefully impromptu about Aristophanes. Our own times would not stand for the coarseness that was one strand in the shimmering verbal complexity that so pleased the Athenians for whom he wrote. Perhaps there was a shift late in his lifetime toward a taste more like ours. What pushed comedy the way it went was surely the taste of the public expressed in the award of prizes. Aristophanes won his share of those, but he was by no means always the champion comic poet. Eleven of his plays were preserved, only because he was thought to be an ideal example of Athenian speech at a time when pure examples of it had become a thing of the past.

Aristophanes is not only untranslatable but almost indescribable. He is like Homer. He is like a snowstorm. If I had just one day of life in ancient Athens, I would spend it in the theater watching a play by Aristophanes.

When the darkness falls, the owls of scholarship spread their wings. But while the darkness was falling on the Greeks—a long process that continued all through the fourth century B.C.—several astonishing things happened. Athens during those death throes, in 399 B.C., had condemned Socrates to death for removing the young from their old beliefs and their innocence. He was almost the last, and certainly the best, of the old Athens. One of his younger disciples, hardly thirty when the master was compelled to drink hemlock, turned out to be a writer of philosophic prose that is one of the most seductive of all the gifts of antiquity. The Socrates of Plato's dialogues is one of the most compelling portraits of a human being that has ever been written down. In all the centuries of Greek writing after Homer, the only human personality that can be known and loved is that of Socrates, yet all we know of him we know almost entirely from Plato.

An Athenian of noble ancestry, Plato thought of himself as old-fashioned, and he liked the company of old men. That is understandable enough in one who lived from 429, the year Pericles died, to 347, when the cold shadow of Macedonian power hung over all the rest of Greece. His life from the age of thirty to forty-two was spent in exile, and the last forty years of his long life were spent in an Athens that was still making all the old mistakes and compounding them with a new social malaise. Those who know the history of his times most intimately do, I think, understand him best—what he disliked, what frightened him. And yet a century and a city in which Plato taught for forty years has something to be said for it.

The dialogues are records of conversations, probably becoming more and more imaginary as Plato himself grew bolder. *The Republic,* one of his most popular large-scale dialogues, begins with a chance encounter that for some reason I have never been able to forget.

> I went down yesterday to the Piraeus with Glaucon the son of Ariston to pray to the goddess, and as I wanted to see how they managed the festival, since they were doing it for the first time. I thought the local procession was beautiful, but the one the Thracians sent was just as good. So we prayed and watched, and then went back toward the city. Polemarchus caught sight of us in the distance and sent his boy running to tell us to stop.

The goddess evoked in this leisurely way is Bendis, a Thracian version of Artemis, and the year must thus be 430 B.C., a year before Plato's birth, when the state established her worship

138

and her festival. Pericles was still alive. The way we think about Athens owes a lot to such curiously memorable passages as this.

The constitution that Socrates suggests in the course of this long dialogue is not democratic; the guardians of law and order inspire amazement in modern readers, and the details of their necessary education inspire horror. I am inclined to think this is intentional, and that their effect must always have been the same. Plato's true solution is not really political at all, it is simply the philosopher king, the apprehension of goodness itself by an individual. But the arguments are subtle, and thirty years after I first read *The Republic* I am still not able to analyze it with any assurance. Maybe I am simply dazed by the charm of a style that sounds so close to a speaking voice.

> And so, Glaucon, the story came true and was not ruined, and it would save us as well, if we believe it, and we shall have a good crossing of the river of Forgetfulness, and not be polluted in our souls.

The most brilliant of the dialogues, and not in my view the least philosophic of them, is the *Symposium*. Once again we can assign it a date. The dinner party it describes—with such convincing narrative detail that it ought really to be called the first novel—took place in 416 B.C., when Plato was only thirteen, four or five years too young to have taken part in it himself, or to have known Socrates as a teacher. This dialogue is the old Athens at its last moment, as Plato most wanted to remember it. One of the major characters is Alcibiades, that brilliant and doomed figure who might almost have come from a Scott Fitzgerald novel. He was then about thirty-four, near the the climax of his brilliant and daring success in public life, and also very near his downfall. The occasion of the dinner party is the victory in the theater by a young poet called Agathon, the first tragic writer to introduce a plot that was pure fiction and not based on mythology. At the time he was probably in his early twenties, and Alcibiades—who bursts into the house at a late stage of the conversation—was in love with him.

Plato wrote long after the event, winding his way into the continuous present of the dialogue through a conversation about old, remote days. The subject is love. Alcibiades later confesses that when he was the most beautiful boy in Athens he tried to seduce

Socrates, in order to have his attention and learn his wisdom. He failed, but Socrates tranquilly proceeded to teach him anyway. When the dinner is over, each of the guests in turn agrees to make a speech in praise of love. The fourth speech is by the poet Aristophanes: a tour de force that makes me willing to believe the whole dinner party really happened, that these speeches really were made. "We have been cut in half," he concludes, "like Arcadia by the Spartans, and only Love can restore our ancient nature and cure us, and make us happy and blessed."

Agathon's own speech is an example of the newest fashion in oratory, as ornamental as a rococo mirror. He tinkles like a harpsichord, balancing word with word, phrase with phrase, sentence with sentence, like a whole orchestra of harpsichords. An astonishing performance, delightful and moving at once, it is also a masterpiece of parody, full of Plato's own quiet amusement: "...banisher of wildness, bestower of concord, giftless of discord, mercifully benignant, wonder of the wise, marvel of the gods..." When it is finished, Socrates makes his contribution, a short but substantial one that might well have been the climax of the work. But at the moment Socrates has reached his gentle and serious conclusion, Alcibiades arrives again with flutes and flowers in honor of Agathon. It may be that so uproarious a personality had to be reserved for this late stage in order to give Socrates his say in peace. What finally collapses, while Alcibiades goes on talking in praise of Socrates, is the dinner party itself. Some of the guests have gone home, some have fallen asleep and awakened again with the cocks at dawn.

> And when he woke he saw the others had fallen asleep or gone home, and only Agathon and Aristophanes and Socrates were still awake and drinking from an enormous bowl which they were circulating. Socrates was talking. Aristodemos said he didn't remember what was said, not having heard the beginning and being drowsy, but the sum of it is that Socrates was compelling them to admit that writing comedies and writing tragedies demanded one and the same man, and the art of tragic poets made them comic poets. When they were forced to that conclusion, and not following any too well, they dozed off; Aristophanes shut his eyes first, and when the sky was bright so did Agathon. Socrates, having put them to sleep, rose and left, and went his usual way, off to the gymnasium, and washed, and spent the day like any other, and wandered home to rest in the evening.

Socrates at the time of that dinner party would have been fifty-three. It was almost the last year in which Athens looked victorious in the war with Sparta; a year later the expedition sailed for Sicily. Alcibiades was murdered in Phrygia at the age of forty-eight. Agathon died at the court of Macedonia, like Euripides, while he was in his thirties. Of all that he wrote, only forty lines survive.

In the course of the fourth century the rich became richer. Slaves were more and more numerous. Abortive and occasionally successful social revolutions smoldered in many parts of Greece. A confidence that had depended on an age-old social system, and a traditional morality, were being sapped by a new series of values based on the circulation of money. The Athenian treasury under Pericles, fed by the contributions of its allies in the war against Persia, had been the greatest accumulation of riches yet commanded by any Greek state. No small state could ever again hope, by mere valor or mere aggression, to dominate its neighbors. The growth of mercenary armies made that certain. In Italy the Roman threat was still a hundred and fifty years away. Nearer home, competing states played out a chess game—the armies of Thrace, Thessaly, Epirus, Athens, Sparta, Thebes all jostling for superiority. With the Macedonians on their way to becoming the military overlords of Greece, less than a century and a half after Thermopylae, the heart had gone out of any effort to resist. What happened is to my mind the most unforeseen event in all of Greek history: by one amazing stroke of luck, good or bad, the succession of Alexander the Great to his father Philip's throne, at a time when Macedonia had just overpowered all mainland Greece. If it was a dream to conquer the Persian Empire, then at least it had a dreamlike logic.

Alexander inherited his father's throne in 336 B.C. and went to war at once. He began with the liberation of Greek Asia and the conquest of all the naval bases of the Persians, including those in Phoenicia and in Egypt. In the Mesopotamian plains he met an army under the King of Kings himself, and overcame it. A fugitive in the end, the King of Kings was murdered by his own friends. When Alexander died, he was already planning campaigns in the West to rival those in the East.

It is curious that while the gods were shrinking into allegory and metaphor, Greek literature and education and the Greek way of life were being extended farther than ever before. It is even true that Greekness itself began at this time to be thought of not only as a national inheritance but as a culture, an atmosphere, and an education, something that could be transferred. Aristotle, a clear-eyed natural scientist, historian, and philosopher, lived through the worst years, and—as the tutor of Alexander—near the center of the storm. Greek geometry is still what we learn at school. Even Greek medicine killed fewer people than any other medicine would do until the nineteenth century. And the Christian Gospels were written in Greek. It was not only the owls that spread their wings.

Oratory flourished in the fourth century, filling the desolation with fireworks. Personally I find most of it unreadable, but there is no denying its enormous influence on the relatively recent oratory of Europe and America—most of which, also, I find unreadable. Poetry was altered; the best poems in Greek for more than a hundred years were small musical epigrams, like the dying twang of classical guitar music.

One of the most interesting of the small poets was a woman, Anyte of Tegea in the plains of Arcadia. She probably wrote about 300 B.C. and she was much moved by what she observed of children and their pets.

> *The child Myro made this tomb*
> *for her grasshopper, a field-nightingale,*
> *and her cicada that lived in the trees,*
> *and she cried because pitiless Death*
> *had taken both of her friends.*

> —(SALLY PURCELL)

The tradition of having pet crickets or grasshoppers has lasted in some villages until very recently. In Maina, in southern Greece, within my own memory, children used to bury beetles with ritual lamentations copied from their elders. A child called Myro has to be a girl, and it looks as if the game of lamentation is as old as the ritual itself. Even the god Pan, in Anyte's pastoral poems, behaves like a real herdsman.

> *"...Why, country Pan, sitting still*
> *Among the lonely shades of the thick-set wood,*
> *Do you shrill on your sweet reed?"*
>          *"So that the heifers*
> *May pasture on these dewy mountains, cropping*
> *The long-haired head of the grass."*

> —(JOHN HEATH-STUBBS/CAROL WHITESIDE)

It really looks as if pastoral Arcadia was invented by Anyte of Tegea, who lived there; Pan was a local god with local sanctuaries and local superstitions. But this long-living theme in literature took time to clarify. Probably the greatest poet in an age of relatively minor poetry was Theocritus, whose countryside was the Sicily where he lived in his youth or the island of Cos. He was writing about 270 B.C., and his poems include epigrams, hymns, narratives, court poems, and a famous urban festival scene. Like most of the Alexandrians, he was a love poet; his characters are love-struck herdsmen, poor fishermen, sorceresses, lower-class Alexandrian women in desperate situations. Of all the translations and imitations of Theocritus—and they exist in many languages—the one that, to my ear, best catches his music consists of a few adapted lines in Milton's *Lycidas:*

> *Where were ye, Nymphs, when the remorseless deep*
> *Closed o'er the head of your loved Lycidas?*

The original runs:

> *"Where were ye, Nymphs,*
> *when Daphnis was melting away,*
> *where were ye, Nymphs?*
>   *In the lovely valleys of Peneos of Pindos?*
> *For you kept not the mighty streams of the river Anapos,*
> *nor the look-out peak of Aitna (Etna),*
> *nor the sacred water of Akis."*
>
>   *Begin, dear Muses, begin the herdsman's song.*
> *The jackals and the wolves howled for him, and the lion*
> *of the forests lamented him dead.*
>   *Begin, dear Muses, begin the herdsman's song....*

The "herdsman's song" appears by this name for the first time in Theocritus, as if the reader would know what it meant, but it has special rules. It involves the singing of short verses, sometimes impromptu, often by two herdsmen alternately in competition with each other, and sometimes with a refrain. It has no literary prehistory so far as we know, but it exactly reflects the rules of singing recorded as folk song among mountain peoples in central

Europe in this century. I have myself heard something very like it both in Europe and in central Asia. So it looks as if here, for the first time, a sophisticated urban poet is making a conscious use of folk song, placed in something like its natural setting.

There are still shepherds and goatherds in the Balkans, though today they often have transistor radios and enormous umbrellas; the singing is over now, and it is mostly the old men who remember the traditional songs. But we need to remind ourselves about the classical world, that it was not all wars and temples. Country people moved about the fields at their own rhythm. Theocritus is still their poet, though we find it hard to tell how many of the jokes and the picturesque lines are his and how many are theirs. Anonymous and popular poetry can be impressive. Homer, after all, was in some sense a popular poet.

The survival of ancient Greek poetry into our time has often been a freak of chance. Most of what has reached us from early Greece is what was chosen for special commentaries and careful editing by the scholars and poets of Alexandria in the third and second centuries. This dusty process was an essential link between the living, breathing, sinful Greece of the real past and the rather sober and severe "classical period" we learned about at school.

And Greece is still there. People still breathe. They make reasonably good wine and excellent jokes. Only a little way under the surface, the same values that were created in the past by poor communications and tough, primitive agriculture can still be found flourishing on the mountainsides, away from the cities. Greece today is not at all Homeric, but if you want to understand the ancient writings there is no better place to conduct your meditations. Personally, I first began to spend time in the Greek countryside because I was besotted with Greek ruins, with ruins of marble architecture grazed over by goats. Then the language, that slowest of revelations, mastered me before I mastered it. In the end I found it was the people I most admired. The Parthenon became to me, as it was to them, among other things just our local castle on its hill. If I became human, it was mostly Greece and the Greeks that made me so.